Praise for Sleep:

'... A gorgeous, gentle book, perfect for young nature lovers...
This stunning information book, with its focus on sleep,
will be a perfect story for sharing at bedtime.'
- Emma Davis, *Childcare Expo*

'Infused with a lovely, gentle humour
and with the added bonus of a factual section at the end.
Perfect bedtime reading.'
- Sarah Donaldson, *Red Lion Books*

'Gorgeous illustrations attractively answer any
curious child's question: where and how do different animals sleep?...
Brief notes at the end provide exactly the right amount
of information to add detail to the pictures.'
- Julia Eccleshare, *LoveReading4Kids*

For Simon and Keturah with oodles of love, expert snoozers.........now! – K.P.

AN OLD BARN BOOK
First published in the UK, Australia and New Zealand in 2018
by Old Barn Books Ltd, Warren Barn, West Sussex, RH20 1JW
This paperback edition published in 2019
www.oldbarnbooks.com

Distributed in the UK by Bounce Sales & Marketing
and in Australia and New Zealand by Walker Books Australia

ISBN: 9781910646274

Printed in Malaysia
10 9 8 7 6 5 4 3 2 1

Paper in this book is certified against the Forest Stewardship
Council® standards. FSC® promotes environmentally
responsible, socially beneficial and economically viable
management of the world's forests.

Sleep

Kate Prendergast

How Nature gets its rest

Cats and dogs sleep curled up…

...most of the time

Geese sleep on the pond,

Chicken in the henhouse.

Horses sleep in the field

…and cows in the barn.

Harvest mice
sleep in
their nests,

Snails sleep in their shells…

…so do tortoises.

Giraffes sleep
standing up.

Sloths sleep
upside-down…

Bats do too!

They sleep all day

and wake at night*.

*we call this being 'nocturnal'

Fish sleep as they swim
and they never shut their eyes

(because they can't!)

Meerkats sleep in a heap…

Rhino sleeps alone.

Tigers sleep in the heat…

…while penguins sleep in the cold.

*Emperor Penguins sleep standing up, with only their thick heels in contact with the frozen ice.

Bears sleep
all winter long…

but ants
only sleep
for a few
moments
at a time.

You sleep too…

And you dream.

Do animals dream?

Did you know?
Some Amazing Animal Facts

Cats and dogs sleep more than us
Dogs sleep for 12 to 14 hours a day, though often in short naps, not one long sleep. Cats can sometimes sleep for up to 20 hours a day.

Chicken
Chicken came originally from the jungles of South East Asia – their ancestor, the Red Jungle Fowl, still lives there. They like to sleep high up on perches, or in trees, where foxes cannot reach them.

Horses

Baby horses – 'foals' – spend about half of their day sleeping until they are three months old. They lie down for their naps. As horses grow older, they sleep less and less and very often doze off standing up.

Cows

Cows usually lie down to sleep and can lie down for up to 14 hours a day. Like horses, adult cows sleep for just 3 to 4 hours out of every 24, in naps of between one and five minutes at a time. The rest of the time when they're lying down they're just dreaming!

Harvest Mouse

Harvest mice are 'cathemeral', meaning they are active day and night, but they are most active in the evening. When a female harvest mouse is going to have babies she climbs up a sturdy corn or grass stalk and weaves a ball-like nest about 10cm in diameter to keep her babies in.

Tortoises

A group of tortoises is called a 'creep'. Not that you see that very often as they mostly live alone. Their shell is made from the same material as fingernails and hooves. They hibernate in cold weather, meaning they go into a deep sleep for the winter months.

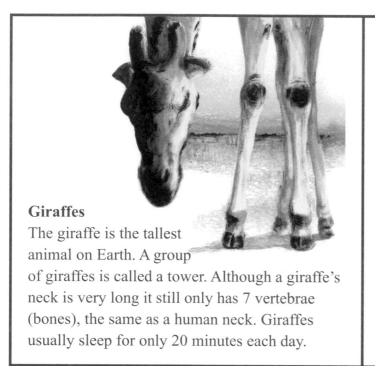

Giraffes

The giraffe is the tallest animal on Earth. A group of giraffes is called a tower. Although a giraffe's neck is very long it still only has 7 vertebrae (bones), the same as a human neck. Giraffes usually sleep for only 20 minutes each day.

Sloths

Sloths snooze for about 15 hours per day, high up in the tropical treetops. They don't move very much, but they do come down from their trees once a week to go to the toilet!

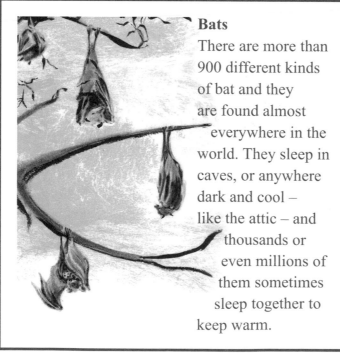

Bats

There are more than 900 different kinds of bat and they are found almost everywhere in the world. They sleep in caves, or anywhere dark and cool – like the attic – and thousands or even millions of them sometimes sleep together to keep warm.

Meerkats

A group of meerkats is called a 'mob'. They live in family groups of around 20, but sometimes as many as 50 live together. While the mob sleeps in a heap, with the the most important female underneath the pile, 'sentries' stay half-awake on the edge, to listen out for danger.

Rhinos

Despite their appearance, Rhinos can run very fast: 30 -40 miles an hour! Their closest animal relatives are tapirs and horses. Rhinos have been around for 60 million years. They doze standing up in the shade in the heat of the day, but lie down to take a deep sleep.

Tiger

The tiger is the biggest cat in the cat family and the biggest sleeper, due to their size. They can grow up to 3.3m long and weigh 300kg. They are great swimmers and can swim up to 6 kilometres. Tigers are an endangered species. There are more tigers kept as pets than live in the wild. NB. They don't make good pets.

Penguins

Penguins never fall into a deep sleep, as they are always on the alert for predators. Instead, they take several short naps throughout the day. Emperor penguins can dive 500 meters underwater and stay submerged for 20 minutes without taking a breath.

Bears

Bears hibernate, so when they awake in Spring they are hungry and hardly sleep at all. By the summer, they start to nap in the daytime, hunting only at night. Bears have the best sense of smell in the animal kingdom. They can smell 7 times better than a bloodhound (whose nose is 300 times better than a human's!).

About the Author:
Kate Prendergast loves to draw all animals, but particularly her rescue dog, Neo. While making this book, Kate was shocked to discover that almost every non-domesticated animal in the book – apart from the ant and the meerkat – was facing a conservation crisis and / or great pressure due to the destruction of its environment by humankind. She hopes that SLEEP will help foster interest in the natural world and its protection.

Also by Kate Prendergast:
Dog on a Train – long-listed for the Klaus Flugge Prize 2016; nominated for the CILIP Kate Greenaway Medal 2017; Finalist, British Book Design and Production Awards, 2016
Dog on a Digger

About Old Barn Books:
Old Barn Books is an independent publisher of picture, gift and novelty books and fiction for ages 9+. We often find our inspiration in nature and from all over the globe.
See more of our books at: www.oldbarnbooks.com
Follow us on twitter and instagram: @oldbarnbooks
Or sign up to our facebook page for updates.

Find out More:
These are some of the websites we looked at where you can find out more about animal habits:
The World Wildlife Fund: https://www.worldwildlife.org/
Save the Rhino: https://www.savetherhino.org
MNN Mother Nature Network: https://www.mnn.com
National Sleep Foundation: https://sleep.org
National Geographic Kids: https://www.natgeokids.com
Animal Corner: https://animalcorner.co.uk/animals/british-mice/